A CENTURY *of*
COVENTRY

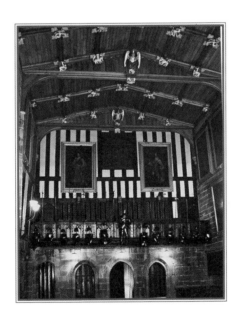

Lady Godiva graces Broadgate Island in the 1960s. The statue is one of only a few in the country to be officially listed. The real Lady Godiva, one of the best known women in the world, was originally named Godgifu. She died in 1067.

A CENTURY *of*
COVENTRY

DAVID McGRORY

SUTTON PUBLISHING

This book was first published in 1999 by Sutton Publishing Limited

This new paperback edition first published in 2007 by
Sutton Publishing, an imprint of NPI Media Group
Cirencester Road · Chalford · Stroud · Gloucestershire · GL6 8PE

British Library Cataloguing in Publication Data
A catalogue record for this book is available from the British Library.

ISBN 978-0-7509-4926-2

Front endpaper: FA Cup Celebration.
Back endpaper: A Christmas scene of Godiva and Broadgate taken by Trevor Pring in the late 1950s.
Half title page: The great hall of St Mary's Guildhall, one of the finest in England. The Guildhall was once
home to the rich merchant guild of Holy Trinity and the seat of civil power for more than 600 years.
Full title page: A Coventry street cleaner takes the time on his evening shift to admire the window display at
Sellrights in the mid-1950s.

For Mum and Dad
Cyril and Beryl McGrory
Time passes but memories are timeless.

Typeset in 11/14pt Photina.
Typesetting and origination by
Sutton Publishing.
Printed and bound in England.

Peeping Tom peering down from the King's Head
Hotel, 1903.

Contents

The ruins of St Michael's and the tower and spire of Holy Trinity Church in the 1960s.

Britain: A Century of Change

Children gathered around an early wireless set in the 1920s. The speed and forms of communication were to change dramatically as the century advanced. (Barnaby's Picture Library)

The delirious rejoicing at the news of the Relief of Mafeking, during the Boer War in May 1900, is a colourful historical moment. But, in retrospect, the introduction that year of the first motor bus was rather more important, signalling another major adjustment to town life. In the previous 60 years railway stations, post-and-telegraph offices, police and fire stations, gas works and gasometers, new livestock markets and covered markets, schools, churches, football grounds, hospitals and asylums, water pumping stations and sewerage plants had totally altered the urban scene, as the country's population tripled and over 70 per cent were born in or moved to the towns.

When Queen Victoria died in 1901, she was measured for her coffin by her grandson Kaiser Wilhelm, the London prostitutes put on black mourning and the blinds came down in the villas and terraces spreading out from the old town centres. These centres were reachable by train and tram, by the new bicycles and still newer motor cars, connected by the new telephone, and lit by gas or even electricity. The shops may have been full of British-made cotton and woollen clothing but the grocers and butchers were selling cheap Danish bacon, Argentinian beef, Australasian mutton, tinned or dried fish and fruit from Canada, California and South Africa. Most of these goods were carried in British-built-and-crewed ships, burning Welsh steam coal.

As the first decade moved on, the Open Spaces Act meant more parks, bowling greens and cricket pitches. The first state pensions came in, together with higher taxation and death duties. These were raised mostly to pay for the new Dreadnought battleships needed to maintain naval superiority over Germany, and deter them from war. But the deterrent did not work. The First World War transformed the place of women, as they took over many men's jobs. Its other legacies were the war memorials which joined the statues of Victorian worthies in main squares round the land. After 1918 death duties bit even harder and a quarter of England changed hands in a few years.

The multiple shop – the chain store – appeared in the high street: Sainsburys, Maypole, Lipton's, Home & Colonial, the Fifty Shilling Tailor, Burton, Boots, W.H. Smith. The shopper was spoilt for choice, attracted by the brash fascias and advertising hoardings for national brands like

Women working as porters on the Great Western Railway, Paddington, c. 1917. (W.L. Kenning/ Adrian Vaughan Collection)

Bovril, Pears Soap, and Ovaltine. Many new buildings began to be seen, such as garages, motor showrooms, picture palaces (cinemas), 'palais de dance', and the bow-windowed, pebble-dashed, tile-hung, half-timbered houses that were built as ribbon-development along the roads and new bypasses or on the new estates nudging the green belts.

During the 1920s cars became more reliable and sophisticated as well as commonplace, with developments like the electric self-starter making them easier for women to drive. Who wanted to turn a crank handle in the new short skirt? This was, indeed, the electric age as much as the motor era. Trolley buses, electric trams and trains extended mass transport and electric light replaced gas in the street and the home, which itself was groomed by the vacuum cleaner.

A major jolt to the march onward and upward was administered by the Great Depression of the early 1930s. The older British industries – textiles, shipbuilding, iron, steel, coal – were already under pressure from foreign competition when this worldwide slump arrived, cutting exports by half in two years and producing 3 million unemployed (and still rising) by 1932. Luckily there were new diversions to alleviate the misery. The 'talkies' arrived in the cinemas; more and more radios and gramophones were to be found in people's homes; there were new women's magazines, with fashion, cookery tips and problem pages; football pools; the flying feats of women pilots like Amy Johnson; the Loch Ness Monster; cheap chocolate and the drama of Edward VIII's abdication.

Father and child cycling past Buckingham Palace on VE Day, 8 May 1945. (Hulton Getty Picture Collection)

Things were looking up again by 1936 and unemployment was down to 2 million. New light industry was booming in the Home Counties as factories struggled to keep up with the demand for radios, radiograms, cars and electronic goods including the first television sets. The threat from Hitler's Germany meant rearmament, particularly of the airforce, which stimulated aircraft and aero engine firms. If you were lucky and lived in the south, there was good money to be earned. A semi-detached house cost £450, a Morris Cowley £150. People may have smoked like chimneys but life expectancy, since 1918, was up by 15 years while the birth rate had almost halved. The fifty-four hour week was down to forty-eight hours and there were 9 million radio licences by 1939.

In some ways it is the little memories that seem to linger longest from the Second World War: the kerbs painted white to show up in the

A family gathered
around their
television set
in the 1950s.
(Hulton Getty
Picture Collection)

blackout, the rattle of ack-ack shrapnel on roof tiles, sparrows killed by bomb blast, painting your legs brown and then adding a black seam down the back to simulate stockings. The biggest damage, apart from London, was in the south-west (Plymouth, Bristol) and the Midlands (Coventry, Birmingham). Postwar reconstruction was rooted in the Beveridge Report which set out the expectations for the Welfare State. This, together with the nationalisation of the Bank of England, coal, gas, electricity and the railways, formed the programme of the Labour government in 1945. At this time the USA was calling in its debts and Britain was beggared by the war, yet still administering its Empire.

Times were hard in the late 1940s, with rationing even more stringent than during the war. Yet this was, as has been said, 'an innocent and well-behaved era'. The first let-up came in 1951 with the Festival of Britain and then there was another fillip in 1953 from the Coronation, which incidentally gave a huge boost to the spread of TV. By 1954 leisure motoring had been resumed but the Comet – Britain's best hope for taking on the American aviation industry

– suffered a series of mysterious crashes. The Suez debacle of 1956 was followed by an acceleration in the withdrawal from Empire, which had begun in 1947 with the Independence of India. Consumerism was truly born with the advent of commercial TV and most homes soon boasted washing machines, fridges, electric irons and fires.

The Lady Chatterley obscenity trial in 1960 was something of a straw in the wind for what was to follow in that decade. A collective loss of inhibition seemed to sweep the land, as stately home owners opened up, the Beatles and the Rolling Stones transformed popular music, and retailing, cinema and the theatre were revolutionised. Designers, hairdressers, photographers and models moved into places vacated by an Establishment put to flight by the new breed of satirists spawned by Beyond the Fringe and Private Eye.

In the 1970s Britain seems to have suffered a prolonged hangover after the excesses of the previous decade. Ulster, inflation and union troubles were not made up for by entry into the EEC, North Sea Oil, Women's Lib or, indeed, Punk Rock. Mrs Thatcher applied the corrective in the 1980s, as the country moved more and more from its old manufacturing base over to providing services, consulting, advertising, and expertise in the 'invisible' market of high finance or in IT. Britain entertained the world with Cats, Phantom of the Opera, Four Weddings and a Funeral, The Full Monty, Mr Bean and the Teletubbies.

The post-1945 townscape has seen changes to match those in the worlds of work, entertainment and politics. In 1956 the Clean Air Act served notice on smogs and pea-souper fogs, smuts and blackened buildings, forcing people to stop burning coal and go over to smokeless sources of heat and energy. In the same decade some of the best urban building took place in the 'new towns' like Basildon, Crawley, Stevenage and Harlow. Elsewhere open warfare was declared on slums and what was labelled inadequate, cramped, back-to-back, two-up, two-down, housing. The new 'machine for living in' was a flat in a high-rise block. The architects and planners who promoted these were in league with the traffic engineers, determined to keep the motor car moving whatever the price in multi-storey car parks, meters, traffic wardens and ring roads.

Carnaby Street in the 1960s. (Barnaby's Picture Library)

The Millennium Dome at Greenwich, 1999. (Michael Durnan/Barnaby's Picture Library)

The old pollutant, coal smoke, was replaced by petrol and diesel exhaust, and traffic noise. Even in the back garden it was hard to find peace as motor mowers, then leaf blowers and strimmers made themselves heard, and the neighbours let you share their choice of music from their powerful new amplifiers, whether you wanted to or not. Fast food was no longer only a pork pie in a pub or fish-and-chips. There were Indian curry houses, Chinese take-aways and American-style hamburgers, while the drinker could get away from beer in a wine bar. Under the impact of television the big Gaumonts and Odeons closed or were rebuilt as multi-screen cinemas, while the palais de dance gave way to discos and clubs.

From the late 1960s the introduction of listed buildings and conservation areas, together with the growth of preservation societies, put a brake on 'comprehensive redevelopment'. Now the new risk at the end of the 1990s is that town centres may die, as shoppers are attracted to the edge-of-town supermarkets surrounded by parking space, where much more than food and groceries can be bought. The ease of the one-stop shop represents the latest challenge to the good health of our towns. But with care, ingenuity and a determination to keep control of our environment, this challenge can be met.

Coventry: An Introduction

The seeds of twentieth-century Coventry were sown in the Victorian period by individuals such as James Starley (father of the cycle), Harry Lawson (founder of Coventry's Daimler) and others such as George Singer (of Singer car and cycle fame) and William Kemp Starley (maker of the first safety cycle).

These are some of the men who contributed to the rise of Coventry as a centre of industry. Others, from the start of the new century, could be added to this list including Alfred Herbert (city benefactor and founder of the largest tool manufacturing company in the world) and Harry Ferguson founder of the Massey Ferguson tractor company, again a world beater, which – unlike many others – has survived to the present day.

Looking up Broadgate towards the National Provincial Bank, 1930s.

The morning of
15 November
1940 at the top of
Trinity Street and
Broadgate.

At the turn of the century Coventry was still essentially small and
surrounded by villages which, over time, have become part of the city
as they were swallowed up by boundary extensions and building. Surges
in population, and the associated growth of the city, was purely due to
the rise of industrialisation which at this time was based on car and
cycle production. The city also had smaller, but thriving, watch and
weaving industries.

The early 1900s saw a noticeable rise in newcomers attracted by
industry. Coventry's Dan Claridge, the last man to drive a stagecoach
from Coventry to London, was interviewed and stated that Coventry
was full of 'foreigners', unlike a few years earlier when everyone knew
him and would call out 'Morning Mr Claridge'.

Coventry in the 1920s was rated as one of the best-preserved medieval cities in Europe but this was not to last for people perceived what we now consider as picturesque and potentially desirable, to be old-fashioned, unhygienic slums. The first major destruction of old buildings came about as part of the laying out of Corporation Street in 1930. Next came work on widening the Burges and Cross Cheaping, High Street and Smithford Street. All these ancient buildings disappeared to make way for the car and ease the flow of traffic as more and more Coventrians became car owners.

One piece of planning which many still find difficult to appreciate was the destruction of Butcher Row and many of its connecting lanes. This row was considered one of the finest ancient streets in the city, especially by artists who created many images of this lovely part of old Coventry. Despite protests, and amidst much apathy, Butcher Row was closed on New Year's Day 1936 and many of the city's finest timbered buildings were unceremoniously ripped down. In 1937 a new street opened to replace it, this was Trinity Street.

In 1938 the City Council created the post of City Architect and 29-year-old Donald Gibson was appointed. Gibson quickly surrounded himself with a team of other young ambitious architects. He was first asked to create a new civic centre and created a plan not only for the centre but also for municipal offices, a library, art gallery and college, all spread within a landscaped area stretching down to Pool Meadow. Ernest Ford, the City Engineer, also put forward separate proposals for a scheme and was the first to moot the idea of a traffic-free shopping area.

As England headed towards war with Nazi Germany, all building projects were put on hold. Gibson found himself designing other structures, such as air-raid shelters and by September 1938 the City Council had begun to dig air-raid shelters in local parks and on waste ground. War was declared in September 1939 and in January 1940 safety measures were carried out in the city for the protection of its treasures. The fine fourteenth-century glass from St Michael was removed and the great tapestry in St Marys Hall was taken down Keresley pit.

Despite all these preparations, no one was prepared for what happened on 14/15 November 1940. The city had suffered minor bombing since June, but that night was a different story altogether. It began much the same as any other although a 'bombers moon' shone brightly upon the city's rooftops. Some people had just settled down for the evening and others were preparing to do their various duties such as Home Guard, Auxiliary Fire Service, Fire Watch etc. when, at 7 p.m., the sirens wailed throughout the city. By 7.20 the bombers were passing over the city centre dropping parachute flares and incendiaries, laying down the targets for those who followed. Hour after hour the heart of Coventry was pounded with high explosives that ripped through the air, incendiaries that thudded to the ground, sometimes flaring up with phospherous, sometimes not. Those who had initially decided to sit it out at home soon realised that this night was not like any others which had gone before. Not long after the beginning of the raid, the defenders of Coventry Cathedral lost their fight with the strings of incendiaries which fell upon its many roofs and soon the cathedral burned. Mains were smashed and those who had come to save the building left, as sheets of red-bronze smoke tore into the sky. Amazingly, the tower survived and so did the clock, which continued to

Mayor, Alderman George Briggs unveils the Levelling Stone on 8 June 1946. The stone of Cumberland granite was personally brought to the city from the Lake District by city architect, Donald Gibson. It marks the beginning of the city's rebuilding and was carved with a phoenix rising from the ashes.

strike the hours, falsely reassuring those who could not see the damage to the cathedral.

The world was stunned by Coventry's ordeal and images of the city were flashed around the globe. There had never been such a prolonged aerial bombardment in the history of mankind. A prevailing memory of the morning after the raid was recounted by the late Eric Bramwell, local historian. He recalled being on duty that night in the Council House and when he left in the morning, among the smoke, drizzle and devastation, he heard a starling singing its heart out, warmed by the heat of the city's destruction, as if to say that the world would go on.

So it did. No sooner had the streets of Coventry been cleared than Donald Gibson was putting forward proposals for its redevelopment. These were heady times for, despite the destruction, the world looked to Coventry to revitalise itself, to be reborn, like a 'phoenix from the ashes'.

By the early 1950s Coventry was the place to be. It had a new pedestrianised precinct, the first in Great Britain, the work of Donald Gibson and Arthur Ling. It also boasted a new cathedral, the first built in postwar Britain. People came in their millions to see it. The cathedral contained the work of the greatest artists and designers of the age – Spence, Epstein, Sutherland, Beyer, Piper, Hutton and Frink, to name but a few.

Throughout the 1950s, '60s and '70s Coventry's population kept rising until it reached 340,000 and then levelled off. This was followed by a decline in numbers due to the slow collapse of the city's car industry and the disappearance of manufacturers such as Singer, Talbot, Standard, Alvis and Humber-Hillman. Even the long-standing Daimler ceased to exist and became Jag-Daimler. The main Daimler factory awaits demolition but the site is to be revived as a new housing estate, once again expanding the population of the Radford area. Coventry's collieries have disappeared beginning with the Craven in Walsgrave in 1926 and ending with Keresley colliery in the 1990s. The Keresley site awaits development as a business park, country park and housing.

As Coventry approaches the end of the twentieth century it continues to develop. A huge entertainment centre has recently opened at the Ring Road end of Spon Street and a new football/sports/ entertainment area has been created in Foleshill – one of the largest in Britain. The Lower Precinct awaits development and, finally, taking Coventry over the boundary and into the new millenium, there is The Phoenix Initiative, which combines Coventry's past with the future. This is truly a reflection of Coventry, a city with a breathtaking past, which forever ploughs forwards into the future . . . an extraordinary city.

A photograph taken in the late 1930s from the tower of the Holy Trinity church looking down towards the Coventry Hippodrome. This area is now earmarked for the Phoenix Initiative and the Hippodrome removed for the building of Millennium Place, a public square standing before a revamped Museum of British Road Transport.

Edwardian Coventry

1900   A wet start to the twentieth century as the centre of Coventry is
flooded. This photograph taken on Monday morning 31 December 1900
shows Queen Victoria Road. During the early hours, around 1 a.m., the
city suffered a torrential downpour and the River Sherbourne burst its
banks. The water poured into the city centre partially refilling the ancient
lake area, once known as the Babu-lacu (The Bablake) with up to 4 ft of
water.

1900   A horse-drawn omnibus outside a Coventry school. As these vehicles had become obsolete by 1900, except for excursions, it seems most likely that this one was on some sort of promotional run around local schools to encourage the use of Birds Powders, which apparently made children happy! It also promoted Birds Hairwash, which probably dealt with unwanted infestations of the head. The promotion was probably sponsored by the well-known Birds Chemist in Spon Street, which stood on the original route of the vehicle.

1902   Looking down Little Park Street towards Earl Street. Amid the refaced brick buildings stands a Georgian town house (recently restored in 1998) and, on the end of the street, the London and Midland Bank, under the charge of Messrs Mellor and Read. Next to the woman can be seen a fine fifteenth-century building, soon to be demolished.

1902   A typical view of one of Coventry's many ancient buildings. Here a woman stands outside her home in Spon End.

1903   Walter and Elizabeth Bates proudly pose in Sunday best with their children outside their home at Court 8, House 5, Much Park Street. Their home was in a shared courtyard, a type of building common to late eighteenth- and early nineteenth-century Coventry. It consisted of one large downstairs room, functioning as a kitchen and living space, and one large upstairs room divided into three spaces to provide sleeping areas. Water could be obtained from a pump in the yard and the toilet was a facility shared with neighbours. Walter Bates was a bicycle fitter at the Humber and later, like many others, joined the motor car industry. The little girl with the bow in her hair was Eva, who married in Coventry Cathedral in 1931.

c. 1903   Looking down Smithford Street towards St John the Baptist's Church. This was probably the second busiest street in Coventry after Broadgate. On the left can be seen the Smithford Street entrance to the King's Head Hotel.

1903   Peeping Tom peering from the top floor niche of the King's Head Hotel. The fifteenth-century figure of Tom had occupied this corner area in various buildings since 1775 and had been peeping down Hertford Street since about 1813.

c. 1903   A fine view of the King's Head Hotel taken from Broadgate. The hotel, which was Coventry's premier guest house began life in medieval times and was extended in the eighteenth century. During this period, and up to the building of Coventry Barracks in 1793, it was the most favoured billet of army officers stationed in the city. The original inn was demolished in the late 1870s and all its fine furniture sold. The new King's Head, as seen in this view, was built soon after by George Woodcock and was opened for Christmas 1879. With the advent of the motor car, its stables were converted into parking bays. The corner of the building was a tap room, remembered by many for its stained glass windows depicting scenes from Coventry's past. In a special niche on the fourth storey can be seen the statue of Peeping Tom. Across the road on the right is the Coventry Hotel, a smaller hotel with an exceptionally fine wrought iron balcony.

1903 A busy Great Butcher Row and Bull Ring photographed in late October/early November 1903. This was once the home of the city's butchers and was known as The Great Butchery. The lower section known as the Bullring (now the front of Wetherspoons) gained its name from the fact that, in 1424, the city council ordered all bulls to be baited here in front of the Priory gate before butchering. Within seven years of this photograph being taken, there was a plan mooted by Alderman Vincent Wyles to destroy Butcher Row and build a new road for easier motor access to Broadgate. It would, however, be another twenty-six years before Great Butcher Row was, sadly, destroyed.

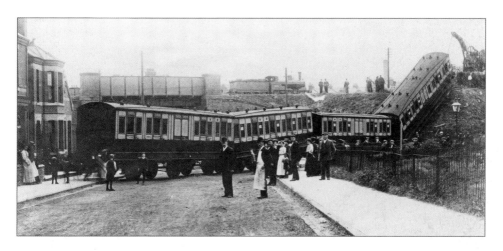

1904 Locals pose for the camera as a crane attempts to winch up a series of derailed train carriages which left the track at The Albany Road bridge which crosses Broomfield Road in Earlsdon on 2 July 1904.

1904 Ye Olde Talbot Inn on the corner of Cross Cheaping and West Orchard. In front of the sign advertising Whitbread's London Stout and India Pale Ale – at 2s 6d a dozen bottles – stands a hackney carriage, plying for fares. Such carriages were soon to be replaced by the motor cab. The 'Olde Talbot' was a refaced timbered building probably dating from the fifteenth century and taking its name from John Talbot, fourth century Earl of Shrewsbury 'The Captain of England' who died aged eighty while fighting in his 41st battle. Talbot was a regular visitor to Coventry, accompanying the royal court of Henry VI.

1905 Daimler chassis being test-driven around St Nicholas Street and Sandy Lane Radford. This was a regular occurrence in the early days of the motor car although, after the initial interest of the locals wore off, it no doubt became more of a nuisance to semi-rural Radford.

1905 Two solid-wheeled Daimler buses full of workers drive past the works offices built in 1909 in Sandy Lane Radford. They are entering the Daimler in Drapers Field, an ex-cotton mill and birthplace of the British motor car which first left the factory in the summer of 1897.

c. 1905   A classic Daimler automobile posed awkwardly across Light Lane, Radford. The Victorian building in the background was destroyed in the Second World War.

1905   Looking up Hertford Street towards Broadgate. On the left can be seen the Peeping Tom public house, home to one of the city's Peeping Tom images. This particular figure was actually a head and shoulders copy of the original 'Tom' in the King's Head. In the middle of the street can be seen The Geisha Café, for many years perhaps Coventry's most popular café.

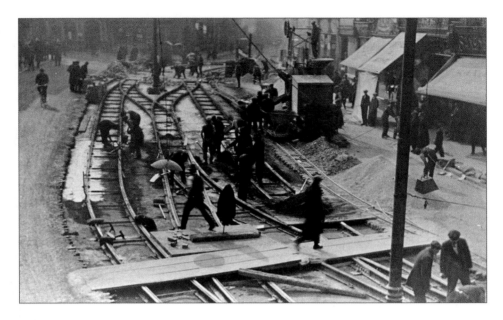

1906   A busy Broadgate leading into Hertford Street. Here the tram system is being extended from the original two tracks which passed through Broadgate. Note how all the cobbles have been lifted – they were later re-laid one by one.

1907   This was the second Godiva Procession of the twentieth century. Actress Patsy Montague, whose stage name was 'La Milo', took the part of Godiva. La Milo was a specialist in living statuary and re-enacted classical scenes, naked and without movement. She was therefore an ideal choice for the Godiva ride although for this she did wear a body stocking. La Milo appeared to have a good figure and also a good heart for she offered her services free in Coventry's now legendary procession. She stayed, as was the tradition, at St Mary's Guildhall the night before the ride and joined the huge gathering at Pool Meadow before leading the two-mile-long procession along a six mile route.

1907 The wheel and pinion cutting shop at Rotherham and Sons Ltd. Watch production had gone on in Coventry since the early eighteenth century. George Porter, three times Mayor of Coventry, being enthroned in St Mary's Hall in 1727, 1745 and 1755, was described as a watchmaker. Watches bearing his name are still in existence. The first major watch manufacturer in Coventry was Vale, Howlett and Carr who began manufacturing in 1754. The company soon became Vale, Carr and Rotherham. Samuel Vale, who lived in Warwick Row, became Mayor of Coventry five times and Richard Kevitt Rotherham did so once, in 1832. By 1860 there were ninety watch manufacturers in Coventry, employing 1,250 men, 667 apprentices and 30 women. In those days much work was done outside the factory in the 'Topshops' of Chapel Fields and Earlsdon, areas almost entirely inhabited by watchmakers. The city suffered in 1860 when the Free Trade Act became law and the Americans put an eighty per cent mark-up on quality handmade English watches being imported into America. Then, as their cheap machine-made watches flooded the English market, local trade was hit hard. Many firms crashed in this period but some survived, including Rotherham and Sons Ltd which continued the production of fine watches and clocks, in its Spon Street factory, into the twentieth century. It stopped only during the two World Wars to make munitions, rifle clips, aircraft parts and scientific instruments etc. One famous holder of a Rotherham's watch, which he used until his death, was Charles Dickens who visited the works in Spon Street in 1857.

1907   A wonderful scene showing Spon End on a warm summer's morning. Hidden below the bricks of these small terraced cottages were medieval timbered buildings, for this was one of Coventry's medieval suburbs. Along this dirt road Kings and Queens have passed and armies marched. Now cars rumble past the only surviving building in the picture, the recently threatened Black Horse (far right).

1910   Drivers, conductors and management of the Coventry Electric Tramways Company pose in front of two trams at the Foleshill depot. By 1912 the company ran fifty-three trams throughout Coventry.

1910 Looking down Pepper Lane towards the tower and spire of St Michael's. On the right stands the Georgian Toby's Head, destroyed in the Second World War. Behind it, jutting out is The Golden Cross. On the left, also now gone stands Francis & Lowney, Gents Outfitters and, beyond, the Governors House which was originally part of the gaol complex.

1910 Trinity Lane was basically a footpath leading between the yard at the front of Holy Trinity and the rear of the buildings of Butcher Row. These lovely buildings, now the site of the flower bed in Trinity Street, were destroyed in 1936. The cottage at the end however still stands and has recently (1998) been restored.

1912 The landlord William Parker, his wife and daughter stand outside the original Plough Inn on the London Road. In the upstairs window a young girl peeps out as the photograph is taken. No doubt she was employed by Mr Parker to clean and serve in the inn. It was the fate of many young girls at this time to 'go into service' in houses great and small.

1912 Tenants being evicted from their home in Well Street which had been condemned by the council as a slum. Note their Victorian furniture passed down a generation or purchased from a second-hand furniture shop. Much of old Coventry was destroyed under the excuse of slum clearance and what was considered a slum in the past is often now a desirable residence.

1912   The Edwardian idyll could be found just outside Coventry at Styvechale Common. Here among the oak and elm filled common land were masses of wild flowers and wildlife, including buzzards, woodpeckers, badgers and lizards. A wonderful playground for these children, two of whom were Bert and Doris Ganley.

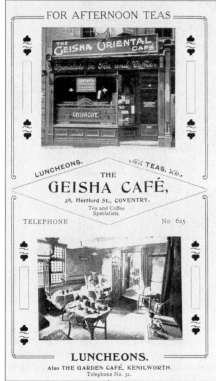

1912   Advertisement for Coventry's popular Geisha Café, 38 Hertford Street. Regular users of the café included children's writer Angela Brazil who lived nearby in The Quadrant. The popular venue appeared around 1901 and continued to be a favourite until its closure in 1961, when the well-liked staff transferred to Gladdings in Shelton Square.

1912 The kitchen of St Mary's Guildhall in Bayley Lane. The guildhall, home to the city's merchant guild and council, is one of the finest in England. Its fine medieval kitchen, comparable with the one at Hampton Court, contains four medieval fire grates each large enough to roast a full-size ox. Here, feasts were prepared for kings and queens. On the buttress can be seen The Knaves Post, an ancient whipping post now in the museum. The kitchen is still used and, sadly, is not accessible to the general public.

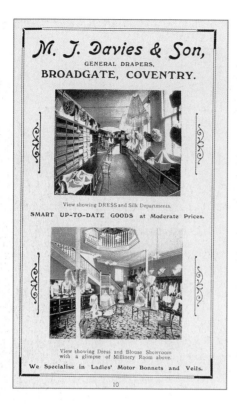

1912   Advertisement for M.J. Davies and Son, General Draper, Broadgate. Davies's stood on the left side of Broadgate, under the present Cathedral Lanes. In their excellently presented premises, they had a 'Dress and Blouse Showroom' above which was the 'Millinery Room'. Davies's, moving with the motor car, specialised in 'Motor Bonnets and Veils' for ladies.

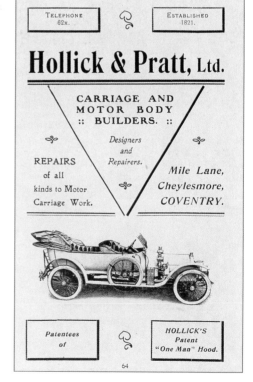

1912   Hollick & Pratt Ltd carriage and motor body builders, designers of vehicles and repairers of damaged vehicles. In this period one was more likely to have an accident with a horse and cart than with another car.

1913 Elizabeth Liggins standing outside her shop, no. 133 Spon Street, with its Christmas display of small Christmas trees, rabbits, chickens and assorted vegetables. By 1920, Elizabeth had moved on, becoming a midwife riding around Coventry on a motorbike, delivering babies. Some of her records still exist, safely kept by her descendant Joyce Street of Coventry. Elizabeth opened her own nursing home in Jesmond Street (off Harnall Lane) but left this after a short time to accompany Lady Barlow on a trip to South Africa. When she returned to Coventry in 1923 she and her husband opened a café in Far Gosford Street. She ended her full days living at Stretton under Fosse.

1913 Holy Trinity Church photographed from the roof of nearby St Michael's. The foundation date of Holy Trinity is unknown but the chancel was in ruins in the fourteenth century. The church appears to have begun life as an exterior chapel of the original priory which was destroyed in the Dissolution.

The First World War

1914   Children enjoying an afternoon in Nauls Mill Park, Radford. Note most of the vegetation is still immature. The pool began life as a mill pond serving Nauls Water Mill for a number of centuries, before being emptied and lined with concrete.

1914   Cook Street, or Tower Gate, roofless and empty, photographed in 1914. On the left is the Tower Inn which was given to the city by the brewery and, despite their wishes to preserve it, demolished by the City Council in July 1963. Cook Street Gate was given to the city by Sir William Wyley after the First World War and has been restored three times since then.

1914   A large group of men pose outside the Broomfield Tavern at the beginning of the First World War. One or two are in uniform but soon this would be true of all men of a certain age. At the outbreak of war, Colonel William Wyley called for volunteers to raise a second battalion for the Royal Warwickshire Regiment. The Masonic Hall was set up as a recruiting centre and thousands lined up. Many lied about their age, including my own grandfather who hit the beach at Gallipolli when he was sixteen years of age. Coventry eventually sent over 35,000 men to join the colours.

1915 Greyfriars Green and the famous Three Spires of Coventry, giving the city its name the 'City of Three Spires'. The green, which began life as Lammas Land, was enclosed in 1875 and landscaped. The cannon in the centre, from another war, was a siege cannon 8 ft 2 in long captured during the Crimean War and brought to the city in 1858. It was scrapped for the war effort in 1943. When the First World War was declared everyone did their bit and those who owned horses had to hand them over for the use of the armed forces. Many people took on extra work to make up for the lack of men in the local workforce. Women had their first taste of the labour market and worked in many previously male-only occupations. Coventry became a refuge for hundreds of Belgian refugees who were initially based in a camp set up at Whitley Abbey. Coventry also became a centre for munitions production and the War Department spent over £40,500,000 here. Various factories in the city and the ordnance works set up in Red Lane produced big guns for the navy as well as guns of all types, bomb shells, ammunition, aeroplanes, tanks, submarine parts and much more. The White & Poppe works, also known as the National Filling Factory, which occupied land between Holbrook Lane and the present Beake Avenue, produced vast amounts of munitions which were stored in underground ammunition bunkers called 'The Dumps'. They were moved out of the site by train which approached the loading bays via a sunken track. The area is still noticeable from Beake Avenue. Guardhouse Road takes its name from one of the main guardhouses for this site. Thirty thousand men and women were brought into Coventry to keep the war effort going day and night. They were housed with locals and at hostels set up at Stoke Heath and Holbrook Lane. The 'Munition Cottages' of Holbrook Lane were a group of 500 wooden huts, mainly on the site of the present park. The threat of air warfare was considered at this time as the Zeppelin crossed the channel. Guns were set up on factory roofs, often impractical as they stood on wheels and were unable to fire straight up. On 12 April 1918 Zeppelins actually dropped bombs on the grounds of Whitley Abbey and on that vital spot, the Baginton Sewage Farm. Searchlights were used and guns in Keresley and Wyken Grange saw action, but no hits. Planes took to the air from Radford Aerodrome but no contact was made. One old gentleman in Woodway Lane is recorded as appearing in his shirt tails and shaking his fist at the Zeppelin while complaining of the absence of police when you need them – so ended the first air raid on Coventry.

1916   An extremely rare photograph showing Daimler BE12s at Radford Aerodrome during the First World War. The airfield was created at the beginning of the war so that Daimler-built aircraft could fly directly from the factory in Sandy Lane. Aircraft left the hangars and took to the air around the present Jubilee Crescent area. The airfield was also used for a short time by Spitfires during the Second World War.

1917   Men producing 15-inch guns for the navy at the massive ordnance works in Red Lane. At the beginning of the war, the works employed three thousand men and the workforce, like the factory, grew throughout the war years.

1918   Coventry lost its first cathedral in 1539. This photograph shows the Collegiate church of St Michael which was promoted to Cathedral status in 1918. Bishop Yeatman-Biggs was made bishop of the newly created cathedral which had the third tallest spire in England. Until its upgrading, St Michael's was considered the largest parish church in England – a position also claimed by St Nicholas' in Great Yarmouth.

1918   The 'top of the town' – Broadgate looking down into Cross Cheaping at the end of the First World War. Peace returned and, with it, those who had left to fight a glorious war which had become a nightmare. England was still rationed for food, coal, gas and electricity and public restaurants were set up in St Mary's Hall kitchen and Ford Street.

1919   On the evening of Saturday 18 July rain ruined a perfect day in which the Godiva 'Peace Procession' had been led by actress and ex-Coventrian Gladys Mann. Unlike previous Godivas, she wore the costume of a Saxon Countess which annoyed those men who had hoped for a more revealing ride. Gladys Mann left as usual from St Mary's Hall and led a procession, including some 20,000 children, from Pool Meadow. The day ended with a firework display which was brought to an abrupt end by heavy rain. Crowds gathered in Broadgate and soon the King's Head found itself under attack from bricks and stones brought by women in their aprons from the Market Square. The police arrived and a running battle was fought in Broadgate and the surrounding streets. The following night the same scene occurred, this time with looting. This was the last time as the Riot Act was read and the city put under curfew. Some say the riots began as rumours spread that certain shops in Broadgate were owned by Germans. These events were not, however, restricted to Coventry – during the summer of 1919 many towns and cities suffered riots, mainly involving demobbed, unemployed soldiers. This photograph shows Broadgate boarded up after the first night of rioting.

1919   All over Coventry and, indeed, all over the land war memorials were being erected to those who served and fell in the First World War. Apart from the larger stone memorials, which survive to the present day, many wooden war memorial plaques were erected such as this one at the Coventry Electric Tramways Company depot at Foleshill. This apparently quiet unveiling was performed by Councillor J.I. Bates who was mayor in November 1918.

Between the Wars

1920   The Coventry Great Fair in Pool Meadow in the 'Roaring Twenties'.
Coventry held a charter for a fair for many centuries and originally it was
held in Broadgate. Later however, until 1858, it was held on Greyfriars
Green and then on Pool Meadow from 1859 to 1930. The Fair was then
moved to Barras Heath and, finally, up to its present venue on Hearsall
Common.

1920   Palace Yard, Earl Street, one of Coventry's lost treasures. Palace Yard stood opposite the last bay of the Council House at St Mary's Lane end. This excellent fifteenth century mansion was built around two courtyards with pleasure grounds at the rear linking it to the Little Palace Yard in Little Park Street which has now also gone. This fine building was, in the sixteenth century, the home of the Hopkins family and it was Samson Hopkins who took in the Princess Elizabeth when conspirators threatened to abduct her from Coombe Abbey during the Gunpowder plot of 1605. In 1687, a year before he fled England, James II was entertained here. James was expected at Whitefriars but chose instead to grace the Palace Yard as Sir Richard Hopkin was a Whig and supporter of the King's controversial policies to reintroduce the Catholic faith into England. The King dined, overlooking the courtyard, in a beautiful room of carved oak panelling and decorated plaster work which, thereafter, became known as the 'King James Room'. In the eighteenth century, the building left the hands of the Hopkins family and became an inn known as 'The Crown'. It had large oak studded doors into the yard which bore the inn's name and the departure and arrival times for stagecoaches. By the mid-nineteenth century it was a builder's yard, ribbon warehouse etc. and began generally to fall into decay. The decay was halted in 1915 when craftworkers took possession of the building and gradually began to restore it. By the time the workshop of Winifred King moved into the building in 1927 it had been restored to its former glory. The future of the Palace Yard seemed assured but no one could foretell its destruction by a single high explosive in the Second World War.

1922   This First World War tank, which weighed 35 tons and had 125 horsepower, was placed on Greyfriars Green in January 1920. The tank, built by the Daimler Company at Drapers Fields, Sandy Lane, was one of forty such vehicles which it produced every week. It was presented to the city by Major General Sir H.B. Walker on behalf of the National War Savings Committee in gratitude for the £8.5 million raised by Coventry during the First World War. The tank was checked by an ex-Daimler tank inspector in 1937 and found to have rusted tracks and an engine which sprang into life at the second attempt. In 1938 it was removed to opposite The Navigation Inn on the Stoney Stanton Road and then scrapped for the new war effort.

1922   The production of Siskin fighters at Armstrong Whitworth Aircraft, Whitley. The Siskin was the first aircraft produced by AWA (who had previously made armaments) at Parkside and it first flew from Radford Aerodrome in 1920. The Siskin became the standard fighter for the Royal Air Force and many foreign air forces. It was the first all-metal production aircraft in the world and won the King's Cup twice, making the name of Armstrong Whitworth famous. Armstrong Whitworth had been brought to Coventry by businessman and aircraft pioneer, John Siddeley, who was looking to go into business to produce his Siskin fighter. He made an agreement with Armstrong Whitworth to move their aeronautical section to the London Road and Little Park Street, Coventry. Later he moved his own part of the industry to Whitley Aerodrome.

Above: 1924   Thomas Whitehead,
manager of the Coventry Electric Tramways
Company, proudly sits before a large
number of his employees who wear their
battle honours with pride. Behind them
stands the company's decorated War
Memorial Tram used to raise funds for the
city's war memorial which was unveiled in
1927.

Left: 1925   This excellent photograph
shows Christchurch's original medieval
tower and spire with its second body. The
first, belonging to the Greyfriars Friary,
was destroyed in the Dissolution and the
second was built between 1829 and 1832.
This, too, would be lost in the 'Holy Week
Raids' of 1941 leaving the tower and spire,
for the second time in its history, standing
alone. The Georgian building on the left
was for many years the Temperance Hotel
but, in the 1920s, it became the booking
office for the LMS Railway with the Cosy
Café upstairs. The building on the right
disappeared with the construction of New
Union Street.

1925 Bonds Hospital (left) was founded in 1506 by Thomas Bond, a Coventry draper, to house ten poor, aged men. The inhabitants had to wear black, in perpetual mourning for their benefactor. They were to pray daily for the soul of the founder of their building. The original tall Elizabethan-style chimneys were blown off in the Second World War and are now, over fifty years later, going to be restored.

1926 Rush hour from Broadgate to the High Street controlled by one traffic officer and an extra beat constable. Note the narrowness of the High Street with the Coventry Arms and National Provincial Bank on the right. Both were demolished in 1928–9 and replaced by the present National Westminster Bank. Cloth caps seem to be compulsory.

1926 Looking down Priory Row to Butcher Row on a warm, still, summer morning in old Coventry. Half of what we see, notably the walls, cobbles left and right and the timbered cottage are still, thankfully, here, gracing the city into the twenty-first century. Beyond the end of the lane all is gone, relegated to the past and to the memories of those who can still recall this time. Priory Row originally led through a lychgate, next to the timbered cottage known then as 'Lychgate Cottage', to the Bishop's Palace. It was straightened in 1807. On the right is the entrance to Blue Coat School soon to become the new Trinity Church Centre.

1926 The hustle and bustle of a busy Broadgate and Cross Cheaping in the 1920s. Cabs wait in the centre as trams rattle up the hill gaining their power from the electrical cables suspended above them which criss-cross Broadgate itself. Both clocks, one on H. Samuel's and one on the wire post in the centre, show the time as 3.40 p.m. and the number of people about suggest that this is likely to be a Saturday.

1926   A deserted Leicester Row near the top of Bishop Street with four interested onlookers standing next to a row of derelict eighteenth-century cottages which were soon, no doubt, to be demolished.

1927   The stark Coventry war memorial raised to commemorate the 2,587 Coventry men who gave their lives for freedom in the First World War. The memorial, which had a beam reaching into the sky, was unveiled on 8 October 1927 before fifty thousand people in the newly created park by Field Marshall Earl Haig.

1927 Armstrong Whitworth Aircraft (AWA) workers pose before the company's second mass-production aircraft, the 400 horsepowered Atlas biplane.

1928 The school leaving age was fourteen years and here, at the AWA factory in Whitley in the press room, are a number of youngsters averaging fifteen years of age.

1929   The AWA Coventry-built Argosy Mark II. This was AWA's first passenger airliner, a biplane powered by Jaguar engines and made for Imperial Airways who operated them on the London to Paris service until 1933.

1929   A white-helmeted policeman stands on point duty at the crossroads of Jordan Well and Cox Street on a sunny day in the 1920s. Beyond the Home and Colonial Stores (right) is the narrow entrance into Freeth Street and, in the distance beyond Halfords, is the tower and clock of the Council House. Apart from the latter and the building set back on the left, nothing of what we see, which includes Elizabethan buildings, survived the bombs and bulldozers.

1929 Miss Muriel Mellerup of Gloucestershire rode as Lady Godiva in The Godiva Procession of 29 June 1929, the first non-actress to play the part. Coventry was packed with thousands of visitors for the procession and 20 extra trains and 400 buses were laid on to bring the people in. Muriel Mellerup chose to play the part of Godiva with some solemnity trying to make the ride more dignified. At the end of the ride, for the first time, a pageant was laid on in the recently opened Memorial Park. Money raised was used to fund the Coventry & Warwickshire hospital. Muriel Mellerup was considered by the press as the 'perfect Godiva' and remained in the city for some time as a guest of the Lord and Lady Mayor.

1929 The first phase of destruction of pre-Second World War Coventry. This view of devastation was taken from what had once been the bottom of Chapel Street and looks across the Well Street and West Orchard area. Amazingly this huge area was cleared in order to lay Corporation Street which opened in 1931.

1931 The old Co-op on the corner of Smithford Street and West Orchard. Only the bottom floor survived the blitz. The store was later rebuilt in the 1950s in Queen Victoria Road.

1932 Trams rattle along as workmen re-lay the cobbled road in the Burges. The left hand side of the street follows its original line but the right hand side has been set farther back by the road widening scheme which began in 1930.

1933 Looking up Hertford Street and Warwick Lane. Curtis and Beamish stands on the right and the 'Peeping Tom Inn' on the left. In the top window can be seen a cast head and shoulders copy of the King's Head Peeping Tom. This can now be seen at the top of Hertford Street. Further along another pub sign can be seen, this was the 'Kenilworth Castle'. Before laying out Hertford Street in 1812–13, Warwick Lane (right) leading to Greyfriars Lane was the original route into the city through Greyfriars Gate.

1933 Looking down Warwick Row alongside Greyfriars Green. Just out of the picture, behind the railings, stands the First World War tank shown on page 49 and before it Sir Thomas White's statue. Erected in 1882, this statue commemorates White, a London merchant who founded a charity in Coventry in 1542 which raises money to this day.

1934 The statue of Peeping Tom was taken from its fourth storey nook and placed in the hallway of the King's Head, the intention being to replace it with a head and shoulders copy. This oak fifteenth-century figure is thought originally to have represented St George, England's Coventry-born saint. The figure is first mentioned in 1658 looking from a window near the Coventry Cross. It has since been in various locations and can now be found in Cathedral Lanes, a short distance from its original site.

1935 Hundreds of completed cars await final inspection at Armstrong Siddeley's Burlington factory.

1935   Looking down the nave of St Michael's towards the Great East Window. This wonderful building was considered by Sir Christopher Wren to be an 'architectural masterpiece'. Five years later it all lay in ruins.

1935   A woman strolls down Little Butcher Row towards Cross Cheaping while J. Hollins, the hairdresser specialising in 'Marcel waves', cleans his windows. Soon all this whole area would fall to the developers.

1935   It was declared that The Butcher Row was to be demolished later this year. The residents prepared for the inevitable and the shops sold off their stock. The buildings on the left follow the line of the present flower bed in Trinity Street.

1936   A stunning scene, beneath the beauty of the churches. The medieval heart of Coventry is ripped out. On New Year's Day 1936 both ends of Butcher Row, Coventry's best surviving medieval street, were closed and Alderman C. Payne, before a small crowd, declared this 'blot on the city' to be closed. Soon afterwards the destruction began and hundreds of buildings dating back to the fourteenth century were bulldozed and unceremoniously cast away.

1936 Looking into Broadgate from Hertford Street. On the left can be seen James Walker, jewellers, in the Bank Chambers, built in 1929–30. In the distance, beyond Hiltons boots and shoes and behind a fence, Tomkinson and Sons Contractors were working on Trinity Street, the replacement for Butcher Row. At this time the population of the city was 194,000 people who occupied 49,315 homes lining over 179 miles of streets.

1936 Coventry's Lady Godiva in this year was Frances Burchell aged twenty-two of 58 Station Road, Harbourne, Birmingham. Miss Burchell was an expert horsewoman having been a riding teacher at her father's riding school. The procession, which incorporated the Coventry Hospital Carnival, was held on 27 June 1936. It included people in fancy dress on foot, the 7th Royal Warwicks Band, historical characters, jazz bands, decorated cycles and cycling clubs, historical tableaux, decorated cars, horse-drawn vehicles and manufacturers' floats. The procession ended with Pat Collins' fair at the Memorial Park and the usual firework display.

1936 An advertisement which could only appear in Coventry, 'Peep in at the Co-op'. The old Co-op store stood on the corner of Smithford Street and West Orchard and lost its top floors in the Second World War.

Norman Parkinson, Photograph

ALVIS

To those in tune with modern life, there is no car like an *ALVIS*

1936 Models are priced from £490.

ALVIS CAR & ENGINEERING CO. LTD., COVENTRY.

1936   Alvis were founded in 1919 by T.G. John and produced their first car in 1920. They had works on the Holyhead Road from 1934 and employed many men, including my grandfather Walter Ernest McGrory. In 1965 the company merged with Rover and, in 1967, were taken over by British Leyland, who produced Alvis's last car, the TF 21.

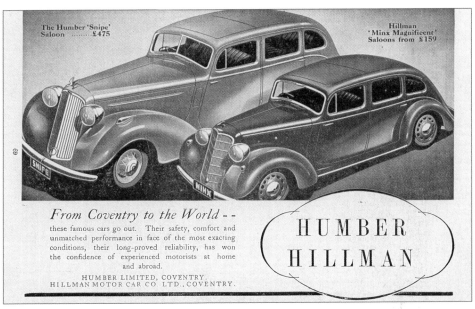

Above: 1936 Thomas Humber founded the company and originally produced cycles at his factory on the corner of Hood Street and Ford Street. The factory burned down in 1896 while Harry Lawson was having the first Bollee car constructed there. The car, or its remains, fell through three floors of the factory. The workers were moved to Motor Mills but soon returned to the original site and, from there, Humber produced the first popular light car, the 'Humbrette'. Production from this site ceased in 1908 and the firm then based its works at the Coronet works in Far Gosford Street. They then left the site due to a fire and set up in Folly Lane, now known as Humber Road, late in 1908. Here they built cycles, motor cycles and motorcars. They also built aircraft, copying the Bleriot machine which flew the channel. Humber was later bought by the Hillman Motor Company and merged to form Humber Hillman. In 1936 there were 7,606 car owners in Coventry.

Right: 1936 Armstrong Siddeley, based in Parkside, began life as Siddeley–Deasey and merged with Armstrong Whitworth in 1918. While the latter continued purely in aircraft production at Whitley, Armstrong Siddeley built quality saloon cars. In 1924 they produced a cheaper range called the 'Stoneleigh'. They also produced aero engines called the Puma, thus giving the name to Puma Road. The company produced their last vehicle in 1960 but continued in engine production.

1936 A painting by Kenneth Aitken, commissioned by Barry James and the Midland Air Museum, of the maiden flight of the Whitley Bomber which flew from Whitley Aerodrome on 17 March 1936. The Whitley was the first heavy bomber used in the Second World War, first produced at Whitley then at Armstrong Whitworth Aircraft's new Baginton works. At the outbreak of war the Whitley was perfected, featuring both tail and nose gun turrets. It had many 'firsts' including being the first bomber to fly over German airspace in September 1939, the first bomber over Berlin and the first RAF craft to bomb enemy targets and drop parachutists. It was also the first British aircraft to sink a U-Boat without naval assistance. The aircraft was the first workhorse of the RAF who were supplied with 1,446 of them. No Whitley bombers have survived.

1937   Trinity Street was officially opened on 16 September 1937 at a total cost of £260,400. In this photograph Alderman Barnacle is addressing the crowd before the ribbon was cut to open the street. After the cutting, the mayoral group walked down Trinity Street followed by the crowd and handed the scissors over to Alderman Vincent Wyles who cut the ribbon at the bottom of the street. Wyles had this privilege as it was he who first came up with the plan for the new road back in 1910, to improve access to Broadgate for the motor car.

1937   Looking down Cross Cheaping into the Burges. On the left can be seen 'Englands' shoe shop and then, in the fifteenth-century building, George Mason who advertises himself as the 'modern grocer'. Mason eventually had a number of shops around the city and ran a grocery delivery service by basket and bicycle, one of which can be seen outside the shop. On the right is the first Owen Owen building, built on Ironmonger Row and Little Butcher Row.

1938   An excellent view looking from the top storey of the King's Head Hotel down the High Street. On the right stands the pillared National Provincial Bank, now the National Westminster Bank. On the left, occupying the corner building, is tobacconist Salmon & Gluckstein, below which is the Glove Shop and the eighteenth-century Martins Bank, originally Atkins and Turton but later the Coventry Building Society, which was demolished in 1989. Across Pepper Lane stand two Elizabethan buildings, the first of which was built in 1587. Both buildings had been recently restored but both would be destroyed by bombs in 1940.

1938   Owen Owen opened in 1937, dominates the lower end of Broadgate and Cross Cheaping. A Coventry-made Daimler bus in the foreground was purchased by the Council in 1935.

1939 At 2.30 p.m. on 25 August a 5 lb bomb, placed in a cycle basket in Broadgate outside Astleys (near Burtons) by the IRA, exploded killing five people and injuring dozens. This was not the first explosion in the city for, over the previous weeks, a number of small devices had exploded in street telephone exchanges etc. After the Broadgate explosion, five men were arrested and two paid with their lives for the deaths which included a man in his eighties, a 15-year-old boy and a young woman choosing her engagement ring from the window of H. Samuel's. The offending bicycle, broken and twisted, is an exhibit in the present 'Black Museum' at the police station, Little Park Street.

1939 Beyond the car is Astley's shop window completely blasted through and its sign blown away. Due to this, and other bombings throughout the county, the government brought in a bill to control membership of the IRA. Soon war would strike Coventry bringing greater terror and destruction than anyone could imagine.

1939   An excellent photograph of a busy Broadgate from the steps of the bank, taken by ex-photography shop owner, James Armer.

1939 War is declared and in Coventry air raid shelters have been under construction since September 1938. In this busy street scene there are only a few reminders that Britain is at war with Germany. On both sides of the street air raid shelter signs can be seen and on the horse-drawn van the words 'Your courage your cheerfulness your resolution will bring us Victory'.

1939 In this scene people pass by the Chapel of St James and St Christopher in Spon End. In late 1939 blackout rules came into operation and, to aid those who could not see in the dark, white paint made its appearance all over the city on anything that could be hazardous. Note here that not only have the posts been painted but also the tree has a white band around the middle.

1939   At the beginning of the war many men left their workplace and joined the forces. Several firms, seeing a labour problem, organised marches by their workers to encourage more women to take jobs in the various industries. Here we see women from Armstrong Whitworth leading the march followed by Coventry Gauge and Tool.

The Second World War

1940   One of the last photographs taken of Broadgate as it was. Soon almost everything in this view would be destroyed in a single night.

1940 The first air raids on Coventry began in June 1940 and on the night of 14 October 1940 Fords Hospital in Greyfriars Lane, one of the finest almshouses in England, was hit by a single bomb killing the warden, a nurse and six inmates. It would be 1953 before this gem of a building would be restored to its former glory.

1940 The Auxiliary Fire Service crew of station 605 cheerfully pose outside their base at the London Laundry. They served the Stoney Stanton Road area, less than affectionately known as 'Hellfire Corner'. Three members of 605 gave their lives to save others and their station was bombed out forcing them to use the house of one of the crew as their base.

1940 Broadgate, on the morning of 15 November 1940, lies in ruins after eleven long hours of non-stop bombing. During the previous night over 500 German planes of Kampfgershwader 100 had dropped 30,000 incendiaries, 500 tons of high explosives and 50 land and oil mines. The pathfinder squadron had flown from France following a radio beam called The X-Gerat System and began dropping incendiaries and parachute flares to mark the target for those who followed. Soon, as the fires converged, approaching bombers could see their target over one hundred miles away. Coventry was likened to 'Dante's Inferno'.

1940 Hertford Street still ablaze on the morning of 15 November. During the previous night the bombers laid a fire-storm in the heart of the city. Some later claimed the raid was on military targets but Hitler had decided to make an example of Coventry in retribution for the RAF bombing of Munich, birthplace of Nazism. On the night of 14/15 November firefighters gave their all – twenty-five were killed, thirty-four seriously injured and two hundred suffered injuries.

1940 The city under martial law on the morning of 15 November. Hundreds of troops were rushed to Coventry to deal with the crisis, keeping law and order, clearance, rescue work, re-laying broken pipe-lines and collecting the remains of the dead.

1940 A converted single-decker bus used as an ambulance passes through Broadgate on the morning of 15 November. The sky hangs heavy with smoke and drizzle as people view the destruction.

1940 Looking across Broadgate towards the Market Clock on the morning of 15 November. In among this destruction twenty-nine relief stations handed out food. Ration books were suddenly useless as the shops were destroyed. Within three days water ran again through the blasted mains, the city once again had electricity and gas quickly followed.

1940 Albert and Elizabeth Asplin survey the damage outside their own wrecked home on 15 November. Before them lies the remains of Eagle Street, Foleshill, hit by a string of bombs. By the end of the war some 56,373 homes were damaged and 3,882 completely destroyed. A total of 1,236 Coventrians and war workers from outside were killed. Many were buried in the London Road Cemetery, some were never recovered.

1940   The destruction of Coventry was headline news the world over because never before had the world experienced such an act of concentrated air bombing on a city. To add to the shock, Coventry's cathedral church of St Michael had been destroyed, not by high explosives, but by incendiary bombs which took hold in the roof space of the north aisle. As the building's defenders, the Revd R.T. Howard, Jack Forbes the stonemason, Mr White and Mr Eaton, tried to tackle the blaze, more incendiaries burned through the cathedral's leaded roof and took hold in the inner roof space. The men, realising they were fighting a losing battle, tried to save various items from the burning building before they were forced to leave. Soon a Solihull fire crew arrived but no sooner had they set up than the water supply stopped because the mains had been destroyed. Liquid lead was pouring down as a policeman and a soldier attempted to clear more incendiaries from the roof. Their heroism had to stop when one exploding phosphorous incendiary blew up, injuring the policeman. Another fire crew arrived and set up a new line but quickly suffered the same fate. Nothing more could be done and soon the building had to be left to its fate.

1941 Coventry suffered two heavy raids in April 1941. Casualties included, as this picture shows, the Coventry & Warwickshire Hospital. The city endured a total of 41 raids between 1940 and 1942.

1941 In September Winston Churchill visited Coventry and made a special visit to the Armstrong Whitworth Aircraft plant at Baginton where he watched a fly-over by a Whitley bomber. Here we see him inspecting a craft from the First World War, a Shuttleworth SE-5. In the background stands a Whitley bomber.

1942   King George VI and Queen Elizabeth in Coventry on 25 February. They visited many places including the cathedral ruins and St Mary's Hall where the King looked at plans for the redevelopment of the city. Here we see them in Pool Meadow sharing a joke with Pearl Hyde, chief of the Women's Volunteer Service.

1942 The bombing of Coventry left tons of rubble which was gradually cleared from the city and spread in dips and hollows in the surrounding countryside. Meanwhile life in the city continued as normally as it could. The market clock tower (centre) was thought to be unsafe and was demolished after falling stonework killed a young boy. The clock mechanism, made by Loseby in 1870, was put into storage and now runs the present Godiva clock in Broadgate. Note the barrage balloons in the distance and the ladders onto the roof of Holy Trinity Church (right foreground).

1942   War production in Coventry was one of the main reasons it was targeted so often during the Second World War. Every firm in the city was geared to such production and thousands of extra workers had been drafted in. Standard Motors made Mosquito fighter bombers, Armstrong Whitworth made Whitleys, Lancasters and Lincolns. Humber produced military vehicles including Scout cars and so impressive were these that Rommel chose to use a captured one for his personal use. All did their part including Dunlop in Holbrook Lane, pictured above, who made wheels and pneumatic brakes for fighters and fighter-bombers. Above we see the gun gear assembly room in which gun mechanisms were produced for the Gladiator, Mosquito, Beaufighter, Hurricane and Spitfire.

1942   A battalion dinner in the canteen of the Humber works, held to boost the morale of the men. On the walls are the flags of Norway, France and the Free French with the Cross of Lorraine. The presence of the American flag shows that this must be after 1941 when the Americans joined the war after the attack on Pearl Harbour.

Above: 1943   Demolition of the first Owen Owen store in August/September 1943. Despite the fact that it had only been open for a few years, Owen Owen's demolition was assured after it received a direct hit from a high explosive and was burned out by incendiaries.

1944   Holy Trinity Church bearing its famous quote 'It all depends on me and I depend on God'. This message was placed on the building by the Revd Clitheroe who was never prepared to lose the building and never did. His belief in protecting it stretched to a request for a gun to be placed on the roof of the building so that he could 'be offensive as well as defensive'.

1945 After almost six years of war Germany surrendered and on VE (Victory in Europe) Day (8 May) Coventry, like the rest of the nation, celebrated the peace with street parties and mass celebrations in the city centre. Churchill's victory speech was relayed into Broadgate by loudspeaker after which the Hippodrome Orchestra played from the Hippodrome steps. In this photograph, during afternoon drizzle, the Revd R.T. Howard gives a service of celebration and prayer in the ruins of St Michael's.

The Postwar Period

1953 Coventry Carnival was for many years the highlight of the Coventry calendar. Here we see the Alvis float passing by the unfinished Owen Owen (now Allders) building in Broadgate.

1945 In 1938 the City Council had decided that it needed an architectural department and 29-year-old Donald Gibson led a young team. As early as 1939 various schemes were being put forward to demolish and redevelop parts of the city centre. Gibson was not the first for before him the City Engineer, Ernest Ford, had suggested a new road system and traffic-free shopping area. The bombing of the city proved a planner's dream and, within a month of the destruction, plans were being made for rebuilding. Both Gibson and Ford put forward blueprints for the rebuilding but only Gibson's was accepted. Above is Gibson's original concept for the precinct, practically traffic free except for cars going along Market Way. The plans were revised later in 1945 as traders objected to the vehicle access and the water feature. Gibson would never complete his grand design, this was left to Arthur Ling who completed the plan, building the Lower Precinct.

1946 Buses ply up and down Broadgate while a huge queue waits at a bus stop. Much of the old shopping area is overgrown with grasses, weeds and fireweed. The Burton building (left) still stands in the corner of Smithford Street (demolished in 1948) and on the old Market Hall site a temporary outdoor market sprang up. Half of the Central Library, with its castellated tower stands on the right minus the reference section which was destroyed on 14 November 1940.

1946 The number 5 bus to Coundon leaves its stop by the Hippodrome. This is no ordinary bus picture because the Hippodrome is not its normal white and appears to be roughly painted, possibly battleship grey, thereby toning down the huge white landmark for wartime safety.

1946 Office staff pose before a Mark II Lincoln bomber built at Armstrong Whitworth, Baginton. Lincolns were built here between 1945 and 1948. They were also brought to Baginton for maintenance and conversion for use in the Far East.

1946   Another
view of a
slightly 'surreal'
Broadgate.

1946   The Armstrong Whitworth 'Flying Wing' glider at Baginton. As a result of wartime tests, the test glider was flown in early 1946 after being released at 15,000 ft over Baginton, first being towed by a Whitley and then by a Lancaster bomber. This futuristic concept first produced by Coventrians, is now believed to be the future of the aeroplane.

1947   The second version of the 'Flying Wing' at Baginton, this time powered by two Coventry-made Rolls-Royce engines. It was covered with a new material called 'Alclad', a metal skin which was later used for the Vulcan and Concord. The revolutionary plane with its 100 ft wingspan could travel at 350 mph. The 'Wing' looked to have a good future until financial assistance to the project was stopped by the Government. Now, in 1999, the American Government is experimenting with another version of the 'Flying Wing'.

1947   A photograph taken in May from the tower of St John's Church, Fleet Street. The building in the foreground still exists, housing various shops. On the right Smithford Street runs up to the High Street, still with many buildings intact. Beyond is Broadgate with the towers of Holy Trinity (left) and St Michael (right).

1948   The demolition of the Burtons building on the corner of Broadgate and Smithford Street on 2 February. This area is now by the Godiva statue in front of Cathedral Lanes, on the bank side. During the excavation of the building which stood where the road is (left of Burtons) workmen digging on the site unearthed a coracle paddle and Bronze Age axehead dating to around 650 BC.

1948   On 24 May the Princess Elizabeth officially opened the newly completed Broadgate Island before a huge crowd. Some have suggested that this was Prince Charles' first visit to the city because, at the time, the Princess was in the early stages of pregnancy.

1948   The surrounds of Broadgate Garden Island photographed as it nears completion in June 1948. Compare this with the photograph on the left and note the road layout. The prefabricated shops on the right, remembered by many, were officially opened on 3 December 1947. Also note the small industrial chimneys which were once scattered around the centre. Despite this, it was noted that Coventry in the 1940s did not suffer like other places with smog.

1949 On 22 October Mrs Lewis Douglas, wife of the American Ambassador to the Court of St James, unveiled the now famous and listed statue of Lady Godiva. The £20,000 equestrian bronze called 'Self Sacrifice' was the work of Sir William Reid Dick and was paid for by William Bassett-Green, grandson of Coventry silk weaver Eli Green.

1949 One could say this represents the beginning of tourism in Coventry as coaches line up outside the ruins of St Michael's for visitors to view the destruction.

1951 Looking across from Derby Lane, which has now gone, over the prefabricated shops towards Broadgate House and the bridge which housed the Bridge Restaurant. Broadgate House was the first building erected around Broadgate and was completed and opened by Lord Silkin in May 1953. The old Empire Cinema stands on the left in Hertford Street which of course, at this time, was still open to traffic.

1951 In the 'Festival of Britain' Godiva Procession the part of Godiva was taken by 28-year-old London student and actress Ann Wrigg. This was the first full procession since 1936 and, unlike her predecessors, Ann Wrigg wore no body stocking.

1951   The Godiva Procession passes along Jordan Well. Ann Wrigg impressed many in her ride as 'The Lady of a Thousand Summers' despite the fact that her horse, 'Willoughby Warrior' was very unsettled on the day. The photograph was taken from the canopy of the Odeon cinema and the buildings in the background, which dated back to the sixteenth century, were demolished in the 1960s.

1951   The procession continues with the two elephants 'Salt' and 'Sauce'. One of them represented the city's emblem and apparently the one behind was not happy unless holding the other's tail. This five-mile-long pageant, which included 1,500 period costumes brought in from London, was considered by many as the finest ever.

1953   The prefabricated shops in Broadgate with Holy Trinity in the background. These temporary wooden and asbestos buildings were officially opened on 3 December 1947.

1953   Despite the fact that Coventry was probably the biggest car manufacturing centre in the country many people still did not own cars and used public transport. This resulted in bus queues like the one above at the bottom of Trinity Street and at many of the city's bus stops.

1953   The Lord and Lady Mayor pass through Broadgate leading the Coventry Carnival in their chauffeur driven, Coventry-made Daimler.

1953   One of hundreds of floats which passed through Broadgate in the 1953 carnival. The carnival was a big event in those days, due to the participation of the city's many hundreds of manufacturing firms.

1953 This excellent photograph, taken by Cliff Barlow, shows the Ferris wheel at Pat Collins Fair held at the Memorial Park during and after the carnival in July 1953.

1953 Sir Alfred Herbert, city benefactor and owner of the largest tool manufacturing company in the world, reopens Fords Hospital on 18 June 1953. This beautiful building, one of the finest of its type in the country, was restored after a single high-explosive badly damaged it. Tiles and wood from the destroyed rear of the building were used in the restoration. It was discovered, during the work, that a large proportion of the building was teak, a rare commodity except in coastal regions.

1954 Gibson's plans get under way. In 1948 the upper part of Smithford Street was closed and the demolition men moved in. Broadgate House (right) was the first building completed (opened in May 1953). Marks & Spencer (left), which opened in April 1954, stands below the White Lion, the only original building standing in Smithford Street. Behind the White Lion stands a huge drill and a crane, while work continues apace on further shops and the Hotel Leofric.

1954 After the destruction of the old cathedral, the city council held a competition to design a new cathedral which resulted in more than 210 entries from all over the world. The winning entry announced in August 1951 was tendered by Basil Spence. Spence had previously visited the ruined cathedral and had a vision of 'a new cathedral growing out of the old', and a great tapestry seen through an engraved glass wall. Spence's design was blasted as a 'monstrosity' and for years after he lost work because of it. Work officially began on the new cathedral on 8 June 1954. The photograph shows the beginning of deep excavations for the building's undercroft in what was originally the graveyard of the old cathedral.

1955   The Upper Precinct represented another first for Coventry, namely the first traffic-free shopping centre in Britain. Donald Gibson didn't stay to see the end result of his plans as he left to work at the War Office. He was replaced by Arthur Ling who completed the Lower Precinct and surrounding areas.

1956   Rehearsals for the Christmas pantomime with the Coventry Hippodrome Orchestra led by Bill Pethers.

1957   Another full dress rehearsal at the Coventry Hippodrome known as the 'Showplace of the Midlands'. The Hippodrome became the Coventry Theatre and continued to entertain local people with hundreds of star names up until the 1980s. It now awaits demolition.

1957   On 23 May Pearl Hyde became the first woman to become Lord Mayor of Coventry. The ceremony in St Mary's Guildhall, the scene of mayoral enthronement since 1342, was also broadcast on national television. This picture shows the previous year's Lord Mayor, Alderman W.I. Thompson, placing the chain of office around her neck.

1957   Lord Iliffe lays the foundation stone of the new Coventry Evening Telegraph building in Corporation Street on 21 November 1957. The Iliffe newspaper empire was started by William Isaac Iliffe who launched the Midland Daily Telegraph in 1891. He died in 1917 and was succeeded by his sons William Coker and Edward. In 1933, Edward was made the first Lord Iliffe. The Midland Daily Telegraph became the Coventry Evening Telegraph during the Second World War. Lord Iliffe stood down as chairman late in 1957 and his son, Langton Iliffe, took over the role.

1957   Home time, as workers leave Armstrong Whitworth Aircraft in Baginton. Similar scenes were repeated all over the city.

1957 The new cathedral was built by Laing who began by laying 670 concrete piles which descended 30 ft into the ground. The undercroft was then constructed and, by early 1957, the 3 ft thick walls were beginning to grow and the outline of the cathedral could be made out.

1958 Coventry airshows were once a popular attraction for Coventrians. Here we see a Shackleton bomber, with its bomb doors open, passing over the airport tower.

1958 Massey Ferguson workers producing the TE20, affectionately known as the 'little grey fergie' at the Banner Lane plant in Tile Hill. The company produced over 500,000 of these small tractors before they were replaced by the FE35. The company was set up by Irishman Harry Ferguson who designed the first tractor that was literally able to grip the ground and transfer the pressure into the plough. In 1946 Ferguson made an agreement with the Standard Motor Company who owned the 'Shadow Factory' in Banner Lane to base his factory here. In 1953 Ferguson merged with Massey Harris of Canada and the company became Massey Ferguson in 1958. 'Masseys' became the largest tractor factory in the western world and continue to export tractors all over the globe today.

Into the 1960s
and '70s

1960 The Coventry built Armstrong Whitworth Aircraft Argosy
transporter, one of 73 built at Baginton. The aeroplane's capacity is being
demonstrated showing that it was able to hold eight Minis.

1961   Subways were very much a part of Broadgate, taking people underground across Hertford Street, as in the photograph, and Trinity Street. Many well remember these long, tiled, sweeping, echoing passages which were a favourite of children who would run down them.

1962   The main office and tower of Courtaulds, Little Heath. Courtaulds was established in the city in 1904. The company, which began life as Huguenot silk throwsters, later made its name with many 'firsts' such as nylon, viscose and rayon.

1962 After years of work, Coventry's new cathedral is finally completed and here we see Queen Elizabeth II at the Service of Consecration in the new Cathedral of St Michael on 25 May. She is preparing to sign as a witness to the bishop's signature on the Sentence of Consecration. Behind her sit Princess Margaret and Lord Snowdon.

1965   Godiva graces Broadgate Garden Island, once a sacred sward of grass on which Coventrians dared not tread. Occasionally, much to everyone's horror, teenagers sunbathed on the grass.

1966   One of the last of the steam trains passes along the 'Coventry avoiding Loopline'. This was on the Foleshill branch line which is now part of the Phoenix Way road system.

1967   Coventry carnivals still continued as part of the yearly calendar. Here we see the Courtaulds float in Broadgate depicting Dr Who's 'Tardis' and his most feared enemy, 'The Daleks'.

1968   At this time vehicles still passed under the Bridge Restaurant which straddles Hertford Street as it had not yet been pedestrianised. Trevor Tennant's Godiva wobbles by under the leering gaze of Peeping Tom as the clock strikes ten. The mechanism for the clock was originally electric put proved unreliable and it is now powered by Edward Loseby's mechanism made in 1870.

COVENTRY INNER RING ROAD
COMPLETION OF DELIVERY
LAST OF 1476 BEAMS
SUPPLIED TO Messrs. GALLIFORD & SONS Ltd., BY DOW MAC Ltd.

1969   The date is 28 June and fifty men and one woman are celebrating the lowering into position of the last concrete beam on stage five of the Inner Ring Road. The 50-ton beam was the 1,476th used and was lowered into place by two giant cranes. The completed ring road totally encircled the city and has proved useful for reducing congestion in the city centre.

1970 The Lunt Roman Fort at Baginton is one of the most important archaeological sites in the country. What makes it particularly special is that it probably had not one but two 'gyri' or horse battle training rings which are the only known ones in western Europe. The fort was occupied by Roman legions on and off over a long period of time between 60–260 AD. Here we see the Royal Engineers in the summer, rebuilding the east gate 'in situ' after having created turf ramparts during the spring in the Roman manner, as seen on Trajan's Column. The gateway was completed in three days.

1973 Royal Engineers reconstructing the Roman granary in its original post holes, using joints recorded from other military sites. The excavation and interpretation of the site was under the control of the Herbert Art Gallery and Museum. Much of the work on the site was carried out originally by Brian Hobley and, for many years after him down to the present day by Margaret Rylatt.

113

1978   People wander around Broadgate in the June sunshine. The area at this time is well-remembered as an oasis of grass, plants and trees. In the background the area with the small trees had been excavated and many medieval dwellings found. Beyond is the old Central Library and the Corporation Canteen.

Modern Coventry

1982   June 2 saw the arrival of Pope John Paul II at Baginton airport
during his tour of Great Britain. An estimated 350,000 gathered at the
airport to receive the pope's blessing. This is a rare scene indeed for John
Paul is the only pope to have ever visited our area.

1987   For some Coventrians this was the most important event in the twentieth century when Coventry City Football Club, led by ex-city player George Curtis and John Sillet, beat the red-hot favourites Tottenham Hotspur in the FA Cup final at Wembley. Here a happy Brian Kilcline raised the FA Cup to the deafening roar of the fans. Steve Ogrizavic and Glen Downs stand behind, arms raised, acknowledging the crowd.

1990   Cathedral Lanes, built upon a large part of old Broadgate, nears completion with the erection of the 'tent' which is liked by some, loathed by others. The project, backed by Saudi Arabian money, has had a chequered history and has never had a full complement of units occupied. This was partially remedied when the Wilkinsons store took over a large part of the building – a necessary solution as the initial idea of creating small specialist shops never quite materialised.

1994   The 'New' Cathedral is a main attraction for visitors to Coventry. Although it is now almost forty years since it was completed, they still keep coming. Epstein's 'St Michael and the Devil' is as powerful as ever, and leaves a deep impression on those who see it.

1995   Her Majesty the Queen, accompanied by Prince Philip, came to Coventry on 13 April to distribute Maundy Money at St Michaels, the 'New Cathedral'. One hundred and thirty eight local people were chosen to receive a purse of Maundy Money, the first time this had happened in the history of the city. Here, in St Marys Hall, the Queen shares a moment with the then Lord Mayor, Councillor Nick Nolan, who had just presented Her Majesty with a cut glass rose bowl.

1997   Pru Poretta, Coventry's official Lady Godiva. Pru first took on the Godiva role when her mother suggested she could play the part after hearing of it on the radio. Pru was initially sceptical but went for an interview where she found out that what was needed was a 'dignified Godiva'. She has since ridden as the lady seven times in major processions since June 1982. Over the years Pru has done much voluntary work as Godiva and also works as an official city guide. She recently received the Coventry Rotary Service Award for 'service above self'. Here we see Pru, uncharacteristically wearing a dark wig, in Hay Lane at the beginning of the 1997 Godiva Pageant.

1997   West Orchards was named after part of the long-gone St Mary's Priory orchard land. The £50 million shopping centre took nearly a million man-hours to complete. One hundred and eighty workmen and engineers worked on the project and 2,000 architects' drawings were made. The glass typanteum is one of the largest in Europe measuring 30 metres wide and 10 metres high.

1999 An extremely rare W2-700 jet engine, one of the first in the world, created by Sir Frank Whittle who was born in 1907 in Newcome Road, Earlsdon. Sir Frank, a creative genius, is the father of the 'jet age'. Through his invention he shrunk the world. The Frank Whittle exhibition is part of a much larger collection of exhibits at the self-funding Midland Air Museum and Sir Frank Whittle Heritage Centre at Baginton.

1999 Part of the Jaguar stand, Coventry's most famous marque at the Museum of British Road Transport in Hales Street. The ever-growing museum is one of the largest collections in the country, boasting more than 190 cars on show, 75 motor cycles and 200 cycles, all made in Coventry. Other things of interest are the blitz exhibition and the excellent Thrust II, the 633 mph record breaking car.

1999 Coventry is an ever-changing city and, as we cross into the new millennium, a new multi-million pound 'Phoenix Initiative' has began. The scheme consists of public squares, gardens and shops, which will sweep down the hillside from Holy Trinity to Lady Herbert's Gardens. The latter will be enlarged. On Hilltop it will expose and interpret the site of the long-gone St Mary's Priory and restore the priory tower and weavers' factory next door. This will overlook gardens and an interpretation centre.

1999 The most controversial part of the millennium initiative, because it requires the demolition of the Coventry Hippodrome, will be Millennium Place, a large open Plaza which will have, set into the ground, an illuminated world clock based on those seen on old radios. This will be unique and will be a reflection of time, which is what the millennium is all about. The museum of British Road Transport will also become more prominent as seen in the artist's impression. Also from here, sweeping across Lady Herbert's Garden, will be something few people have seen before, a glass bridge walkway. So, at the end of the century, Coventry steps, once again, into new times and new developments.

Acknowledgements

I would like to thank the following for supplying me with the photographs for this book. Coventry Evening Telegraph (Dan Mason, June Weatherfield); Midland Air Museum (Barry James); Herbert Art Gallery & Museum (Margaret Rylatt); Museum of British Road Transport (Barry Littlewood); Coventry City Council Phoenix Initiative (Moore Flannerly); Dunlop Aviation (Diane Plunkett); Cliff Barlow, Roger Bailey, John Ashby, John Stanton, Pru Poretta, Trevor Pring, Joyce Street, Sheila Martin, Les Fannon, James Armer, Norman Parkinson, J&H Buust, Kenneth Aitken. Everything has been done to trace the copyright holders of photographs and I apologise to anyone I have not credited. Special thanks also go to Heather for her hard work which made it possible for this book to be produced in record time.